The Big Adventures of
LITTLE "LUCKY"

Book 1 of THE RESCUE SERIES

PAULA GEHRING-KEVISH

PAGE PUBLISHING, INC.
Conneaut Lake, PA

First originally published by Page Publishing 2020

ISBN 978-1-64584-459-4 (pbk)
ISBN 978-1-64584-461-7 (hc)
ISBN 978-1-64584-460-0 (digital)

Printed in the United States of America

To my parents who taught me compassion,

kindness and empathy towards animals

—Paula Kevish

It was summertime in Las Vegas, Nevada. The daytime temperature reached over one hundred degrees.

Lucky was found in the backyard of a deserted house with an almost-empty bag of food and very little water. Lucky was very thin.

But Lucky wasn't sad; his tail was wagging! Lucky's tail is *always* wagging! Lucky spent his first day, on the way to his new home, riding in the truck with Dad. He had his paws perched up on the dashboard, tongue hanging out, and yes, his tail was wagging.

When he came home to meet his mom, the boys, and his new sister, Gracie, guess what? You got it, his tail was wagging!

One day, Lucky was walking funny, so we took him to see the pet doctor. They told us Lucky could not move his back legs. Lucky's tail was not moving either.

Lucky had a lot of work ahead of him. Even though he could not move his back legs, he would use his front legs to crawl over to us, roll over, and wait for a tummy rub.

It took a long time and a lot of physical therapy, but one day, Lucky's dad called and said, "Guess what? Lucky just wagged his tail!"

Even though Lucky has a "funny" walk, he gets around just fine. He and Gracie play every day.

Lucky even gets to take rides in Dad's truck again. He is a celebrity everywhere he goes!

Lucky loves his trips to the local hardware store where everyone knows him by name. They even have treats waiting for him when he visits on Sundays.

And guess what? Lucky's tail is still wagging, and he has a new brother named Gunner.

ABOUT THE AUTHOR

Paula Gehring-Kevish holds a bachelor of science degree as well as a master's degree in school counseling. Two of her passions are animals and children. *The Rescue* series offers her the chance to write about animals for children. She currently resides in Las Vegas, Nevada, with her husband, Steve. In addition, she has two sons and three grandchildren.

CPSIA information can be obtained
at www.ICGtesting.com
Printed in the USA
JSHW010554190421
13664JS00001B/5

9 781645 844594